P9-DEG-678

BLOOMINGTON
PUBLIC LIBRARY

MAR 1 1

SandCastle™

First Sounds

Sara and Sam

Anders Hanson

Consulting Editor, Diane Craig, M.A./Reading Specialist

ABDO
Publishing Company

Published by ABDO Publishing Company, 4940 Viking Drive, Edina, Minnesota 55435.

Copyright © 2005 by Abdo Consulting Group, Inc. International copyrights reserved in all countries. No part of this book may be reproduced in any form without written permission from the publisher. SandCastle™ is a trademark and logo of ABDO Publishing Company.

Printed in the United States.

Credits
Edited by: Pam Price
Curriculum Coordinator: Nancy Tuminelly
Cover and Interior Design and Production: Mighty Media
Child Photography: Steven Wewerka, Wewerka Photography
Photo Credits: AbleStock, Comstock, John Foxx, Photodisc

Library of Congress Cataloging-in-Publication Data

Hanson, Anders, 1980-
    Sara and Sam / Anders Hanson.
        p. cm. -- (First sounds)
    Includes index.
    ISBN 1-59679-188-8 (hardcover)
    ISBN 1-59679-189-6 (paperback)
        1. English language--Consonants--Juvenile literature. I. Title. II. Series.

PE1159.H364 2005
428.1'3--dc22
                                                                    2004056865

SandCastle™ books are created by a professional team of educators, reading specialists, and content developers around five essential components that include phonemic awareness, phonics, vocabulary, text comprehension, and fluency. All books are written, reviewed, and leveled for guided reading, early intervention reading, and Accelerated Reader® programs and designed for use in shared, guided, and independent reading and writing activities to support a balanced approach to literacy instruction.

Let Us Know

After reading the book, SandCastle would like you to tell us your stories about reading. What is your favorite page? Was there something hard that you needed help with? Share the ups and downs of learning to read. We want to hear from you! To get posted on the ABDO Publishing Company Web site, send us e-mail at:

sandcastle@abdopub.com

SandCastle Level: Emerging

ABCDEFGH

IJKLMNOPQ

RSTUVWXYZ

abcdefgh

ijklmnopq

rstuvwxyz

Sara

Sam

saw

salt

sack

7

seven

9

suitcase

Look at the  .

Look at the .

Look at the  .

Look at the 7.

Look at the .

Sara looks at
the sack.

Sam looks at the seven.

The seven is in the sack.

Which of these pictures begin with s?

More words that begin with s

sad

sea

seal

see

sit

so

soft

sun

About SandCastle™

A professional team of educators, reading specialists, and content developers created the SandCastle™ series to support young readers as they develop reading skills and strategies and increase their general knowledge. The SandCastle™ series has four levels that correspond to early literacy development in young children. The levels are provided to help teachers and parents select the appropriate books for young readers.

Emerging Readers
(no flags)

Beginning Readers
(1 flag)

Transitional Readers
(2 flags)

Fluent Readers
(3 flags)

These levels are meant only as a guide. All levels are subject to change.

To see a complete list of SandCastle™ books and other nonfiction titles from ABDO Publishing Company, visit **www.abdopub.com** or contact us at:
4940 Viking Drive, Edina, Minnesota 55435 • 1-800-800-1312 • fax: 1-952-831-1632